Eye in the Sky
THE HUBBLE TELESCOPE

By Harriet Sigerman

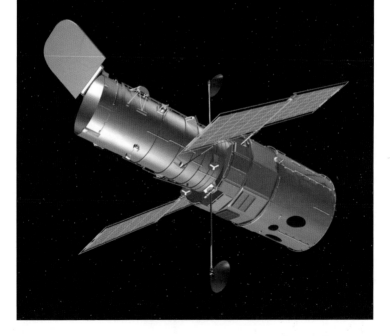

CELEBRATION PRESS
Pearson Learning Group

CONTENTS

"Ten, nine, eight, seven, six, five, four, three, two, one . . . Liftoff!" On April 24, 1990, the sleek, white spacecraft roared into the sky, leaving behind a trail of smoke and fire. It was the shuttle *Discovery* rocketing to outer space with five astronauts onboard. This was no ordinary **shuttle** flight. In *Discovery*'s payload bay, or cargo area, there was a long, round instrument—the Hubble Space Telescope (HST). It was ready to be placed in orbit.

The Hubble Space Telescope lifts off aboard the *Discovery* space shuttle.

Around the world, people interested in space exploration followed *Discovery's* path as it soared out of Earth's atmosphere. The HST was the beginning of a new era in exploring our universe.

The Hubble Space Telescope

Hubble would orbit Earth and send back images of outer space. Scientists hoped that Hubble would help to answer many questions about the universe.

From earliest times, people would look up to the skies and see the beauty of the stars, the Moon, and the planets. People were unable to explain the objects they saw, so they made up stories.

Later, as people observed the sky, they recorded what they saw. They noted the changing position of the Sun, Moon, and stars. They followed the changing phases of the Moon and recorded unusual events, such as **eclipses**.

Gradually, people developed tools like microscopes, telescopes, and computers. These tools helped them gather knowledge about the universe. The Hubble Space Telescope is a tool that also has brought us a much clearer view of the universe.

Since the telescope was invented, astronomers have used telescopes to learn about stars, planets, and other objects in the universe. Most telescopes were designed to be used on Earth.

The telescopes **astronomers** use are powerful. However, they do not have the clearest vision of the **cosmos**. This is because all light from space that reaches a telescope on the ground is blurred by Earth's atmosphere.

The Hubble Space Telescope orbits far above Earth, so it has the best view yet. Since it is not blurred by the Earth's atmosphere, the HST can see more clearly and much farther into space than any telescopes on the ground. By peering into the farthest reaches of space, the Hubble Space Telescope can help answer many questions about our universe. These questions include the size and make-up of other **galaxies** and whether life exists elsewhere in the universe. The Hubble Space Telescope is truly our eye in the sky!

The telescope has a fascinating history. Most historians believe that in 1608, Hans Lippershey made the first basic telescope. Lippershey was a Dutch eyeglass maker. It seems that two children were playing with eyeglass lenses in his shop. They put one lens directly in front of another. Then they discovered that distant objects appeared enlarged and upside down when viewed through the two lenses.

Lippershey used the children's discovery to make a telescope. News of his invention spread throughout Europe, and telescopes became readily available. However, they were of very poor quality.

A year later, in 1609, the Italian scientist Galileo Galilei made a more powerful telescope that he used to view distant objects in the sky. As a result, he made discoveries that completely changed our ideas about the

Galileo's telescope

With his telescope, Galileo changed our view of Earth's place in the cosmos.

universe.

Before Galileo, most people believed that Earth was the center of the universe. Through his telescope, Galileo saw that this was not true. Instead, he saw that Earth and other planets circled the Sun.

Galileo made other discoveries, as well. He saw that Venus had different phases. It looked lighter, darker, closer, or farther away at different times. He also discovered four small, never-before-seen objects that appeared to circle Jupiter.

Most scientists thought Galileo was wrong. However, his ideas and discoveries gained acceptance and revolutionized our view of the universe.

In 1668, the English scientist Sir Isaac Newton (1642–1727) invented a **reflecting telescope**. This telescope was different from the **refracting telescope** used by Galileo. A refracting telescope uses two clear glass lenses. The larger lens collects light from a star or other cosmic body and directs the light to a smaller lens at the other end of the telescope. This smaller lens magnifies the object.

A reflecting telescope uses a mirror instead of a clear lens to collect light. One end of the telescope is open. Light enters the telescope through this end and bounces onto a mirror at the other end. It then reflects back to a smaller mirror, like a ball bouncing between two walls. From the smaller mirror, the light bounces up to a magnifying lens.

Reflecting telescopes have certain advantages over refracting telescopes because mirrors can be larger and more accurate than glass lenses. As a result, Newton saw larger areas of the universe with his reflecting telescope.

Over the next few hundred years, scientists improved telescopes. By the twentieth century, telescopes had grown both in size and power.

In 1917, a telescope with a 100-inch lens was installed on Mount Wilson near Los Angeles, California. It was the largest telescope in the world until 1948. Then an even larger mirror was installed on a telescope at Mount Palomar in the hills near San Diego, California. It was 200 inches across.

At the National Radio Astronomy Observatory in Green Bank, West Virginia, there is a telescope. Its 140-foot antennae scans the sky to pick up radio signals from distant galaxies.

The two largest telescopes in the world are at the top of a 13,796-foot volcano in Hawaii. The volcano's name is Mauna Kea. Each gigantic telescope is as tall as an eight-story building and weighs 300 tons.

Location of Keck Observatory

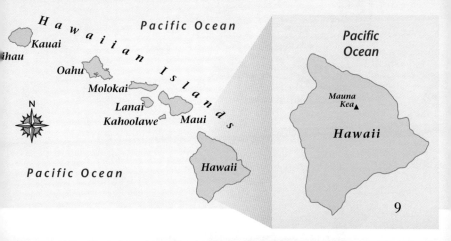

The telescopes were installed in 1993 and 1996. Each of them has a mirror that measures nearly 400 inches. These giants are part of the W. M. Keck Observatory.

Despite the mammoth size and remote locations of these telescopes, they cannot overcome the effects of Earth's atmosphere. Therefore, it is difficult for them to get a clear view of the universe. That is a task for a telescope orbiting in space.

The telescopes located near the top of Mount Kea on the island of Hawaii represent 11 different countries. Keck I and II are located here.

How Hubble Was Built

For many years, scientists wanted to find a way to view outer space from space. In 1923, German scientist Hermann Oberth thought about putting an orbiting telescope aboard a spaceship. At a time when airplane travel was still new, scientists laughed at his idea.

In the 1960s, both Russia and the United States were putting astronauts in space. That is when scientists thought about Oberth's ideas. On July 20, 1969, the *Apollo 11* astronauts Neil Armstrong and Edwin "Buzz" Aldrin set foot on the Moon. Scientists said that if people could walk on the Moon, it was time to build an Earth-orbiting telescope.

In 1972, the U.S. Congress approved a space shuttle program. Space shuttles are large spacecraft that carry astronauts into outer space. Space shuttles can also carry different equipment from small instruments to a large telescope.

The National Aeronautics and Space Administration (NASA), the agency in charge of America's space program, had already launched smaller telescopes. Other countries also sent small telescopes into space. Although they provided important information, these telescopes only had the power to take a "snapshot" of a planet or star.

In 1977, the U.S. Congress approved the building of a large space telescope. In 1984, the project was renamed the Hubble Space Telescope, after Edwin P. Hubble. Hubble was an American astronomer who made important discoveries about the universe.

There were many challenges involved in designing and building Hubble. They included perfecting the telescope's sensitive instruments and making a lightweight structure for mounting the mirrors.

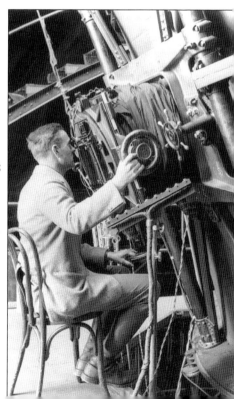

Edwin P. Hubble

NASA technicians building Hubble

Problems with the space shuttle program further delayed the launch of Hubble until 1990. One of the problems was the tragic explosion of *Challenger* in 1986. The project cost $1.6 billion and was finally ready for testing in 1985.

The Hubble Space Telescope is a reflecting telescope that weighs about 24,500 pounds and measures 43.5 feet. It is about the size of a large school bus. The main mirror is almost 8 feet.

The Hubble Space Telescope is built from connecting pieces and systems like a giant jigsaw puzzle. It looks like an enormous flying insect. It is made up of many different instruments that enable the telescope to remain in orbit, "obey" instructions from scientists on the ground, and transmit images. The powerful instruments let scientists look into the farthest reaches of space.

13

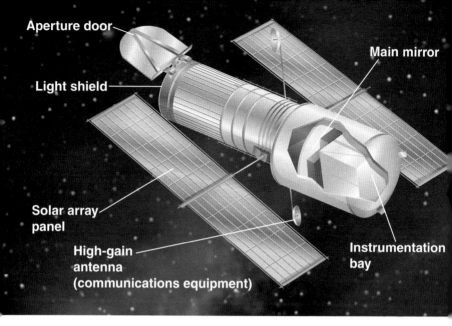

Aperture door

Light shield

Solar array panel

High-gain antenna (communications equipment)

Main mirror

Instrumentation bay

The parts of the Hubble Space Telescope

A Cassegrain reflector is one of Hubble's instruments. It consists of a primary and secondary mirror. The mirrors direct light entering the telescope to a surface that is about 10 inches wide.

Another important instrument is the Faint Object Camera (FOC). This camera can detect objects up to seven times farther away from Earth than any objects seen through the largest ground telescope.

The Wide Field/Planetary Camera (WF/PC) is an important feature, too. It can photograph a large portion of the sky and study all of the planets in our solar system, except Earth and Mercury.

14

A solar array, or panel, is mounted on each side of the Hubble Space Telescope. Each panel has solar cells. These cells make electricity when sunlight falls on them. This electricity powers the Hubble.

How do scientists view the universe through the Hubble Space Telescope? A communications system relays Hubble's **radio signals** to computers at NASA's Goddard Space Flight Center in Greenbelt, Maryland. The computers process the data and send it to the Space Telescope Science Institute in Baltimore, Maryland. Then technicians convert the data into pictures.

Hubble orbiting Earth

The Hubble Space Telescope is not the biggest telescope with the largest mirror ever built. However, it observes the universe from the most ideal location. It orbits about 380 miles above Earth's surface and beyond Earth's atmosphere.

Hubble's most important tool in gathering information is light. The light from stars, planets, and other cosmic bodies tells scientists how old an object is, what it is made of, and how far it is from Earth. Without the light that an object sends out, astronomers cannot find out what they want to know. In other words, they are truly "in the dark."

Light travels at the speed of 186,282 miles a second. It travels a distance of about 6 trillion miles in a year. This distance is called a **light-year**. Most stars in our Milky Way galaxy are thousands of light-years away from Earth. Other galaxies are millions of light-years away. Really distant galaxies are thought to be billions of light-years away.

If a star is 10,000 light-years away from Earth, we are looking at it as it appeared 10,000 years ago. By viewing objects in space, the Hubble Space Telescope sends images to Earth that show what those objects looked like when they were much younger.

The Hubble was finally **deployed** from the shuttle in April 1990. Scientists hoped that it would help them understand how the universe has changed. They hoped that the telescope would tell them what stars and planets are made of. They also hoped that the Hubble would measure the distances to other galaxies.

The day after Hubble rocketed into space, the shuttle's astronauts carefully lifted the more than 25,000-pound telescope using the shuttle's remote manipulator arm. The remote manipulator arm released its hold, and the HST floated free in orbit.

For several days, ground control crews tested the telescope's instruments. They fixed small problems by sending computerized instructions to Hubble. Eagerly, they awaited the first pictures. These pictures came a little over a month later. Hubble's first assignment was to photograph a star cluster in the constellation Carina. The pictures were sharper and more detailed than what a telescope on the ground could capture. However, they weren't the clear and bright images that Hubble was supposed to produce. The star was visible in the photographs, but so was a fuzzy halo around it that blocked out other stars.

Hubble's controllers on Earth repeatedly adjusted the primary and secondary mirrors. However, each image that Hubble sent back was no better. The telescope was out of focus. What had gone wrong?

The controllers soon discovered that the primary mirror was too flat near the edge. The mirror's curve was off by only one-fiftieth the thickness of a human hair! That was enough to affect the telescope's ability to focus exactly. The Hubble needed a corrective lens.

The mirror was too large to replace while Hubble was in orbit. Scientists were able to make the images clearer by reprogramming the computers. NASA also scheduled a repair mission. On December 2, 1993, the space shuttle *Endeavour* embarked on an 11-day mission, with new equipment and seven astronauts on board.

When the shuttle drew close enough to Hubble, the astronauts used a mechanical space arm on the *Endeavour* to capture the telescope. Carefully, they maneuvered Hubble into the shuttle's cargo bay.

As the whole world watched on television, four astronauts repaired the telescope during five spacewalks, which lasted a little over 35 hours. Attached to the shuttle's robot arm, they ventured into outer space to the cargo bay.

They added a new instrument called the Corrective Optics Space Telescope Axial Replacement (COSTAR). COSTAR helped correct the primary mirror and focus light entering the telescope. They also replaced the WF/PC with the WF/PC2.

The astronauts had spent many hours practicing on a model of the HST on Earth. As a result, the repairs were completed with no problems.

Astronaut Kathryn C. Thornton working on Hubble during the repair mission in 1993

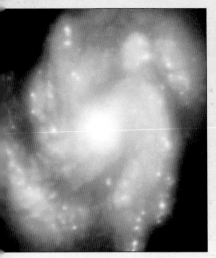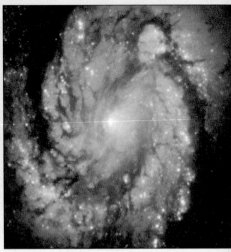

Pictures of M100, a spiral galaxy, taken by Hubble before it was repaired (left) and after (right)

Early in the morning on December 18, 1993, a team of Hubble's scientists gathered in front of a computer screen at the Space Telescope Science Institute. Hearts pounding, they waited for the first images from the repaired Hubble.

The pictures soon came into view. The scientists cheered as a star appeared on the screen. The Hubble Space Telescope was back in business.

Although the repairs that *Endeavour*'s astronauts made greatly improved Hubble's images, the primary mirror was still flawed. In 1997, 1999, and 2002, crews traveled to Hubble to make more repairs that have further improved the telescope.

Hubble orbits Earth every 97 minutes at a speed of 5 miles per second. That is more than 17,000 miles an hour. As it zooms around Earth, it continues to reveal many important discoveries.

In 1994, Hubble's cameras captured an "attack" on Jupiter. Pieces of a comet fell into the planet's atmosphere and exploded. Large telescopes on Earth also observed the impact. However, Hubble provided the clearest and most detailed images of this event.

Pieces of a comet explode as they collide with Jupiter's atmosphere.

The spectacular images from Hubble showed gigantic explosions as pieces of the comet entered Jupiter's atmosphere. These photos helped scientists understand what happens when a comet hits a planet.

Hubble also has taken pictures of Jupiter's four moons. The photos showed spectacular details of volcanic eruptions on Io, a thin atmosphere of oxygen around Europa, ice crystals on Callista, and ozone on Ganymede.

The telescope has taken some other important pictures of planets in our solar system. These include pictures of Pluto and its moon, Charon. It has observed the atmospheric conditions of Saturn and Neptune and weather conditions on Mars. All of this information provides clues to scientists who want to know if there is life on other planets.

Hubble has also produced pictures of the formation of stars. In 1995, Hubble captured the entire process in a series of fiery orange and yellow images.

These pictures show thick jets of dust and gas shooting out from a hidden core. The gas appears to be falling inward, back into the core. Then it rotates slowly and then faster as it draws closer to the star emerging from the core.

Hubble has made some of its most dazzling discoveries beyond our solar system. It has collected many images of galaxies at different stages of formation. The WF/PC captured a group of these galaxies. They are about 7 to 10 billion light-years away from Earth. They probably formed when the universe was much younger.

Hubble has also recorded images of older galaxies growing larger and changing shape. It has taken photographs of galaxies combining and of galaxies colliding.

By focusing on faint objects that might be very young galaxies, Hubble is helping astronomers gaze back into the earliest age of the universe. They can look closer at the explosion that some people believe began our universe. This is nicknamed the Big Bang Theory.

This image from Hubble shows two spiral galaxies colliding. As the galaxies collided, two curved streams of star flung into intergalactic space. The collision spurred the birth of new stars in each galaxy.

In January 2003, researchers reported that the Hubble telescope had located objects from a time approximately a billion years after the Big Bang. During this period, millions of stars in the universe emerged.

A billion years may seem like a very long time. However, it's barely a mega-second in cosmic time. With Hubble's help, astronomers are now creating a picture of how the universe looked soon after it first appeared.

For many years, astronomers have thought that the universe is like a kind of cosmic Swiss cheese. This is because it is full of black holes. These are small areas in space that contain dense matter and intense gravity. This intense force pulls in even light, like a vacuum cleaner sucks up dust. Black holes occur when enormous stars die, and their mass compacts into a small area.

Hubble helped prove that these dense areas exist. In 1997, the Hubble Space Telescope provided images that showed a doughnut-shaped structure made of dust and gas. Hubble had located a black hole! The data told scientists that black holes exist in the center of many galaxies. We now know that black holes are widespread throughout the universe.

This picture of a black hole shows an enormous disk circling around a black hole in the center of a faraway galaxy.

The glowing remains of a dying star

The Hubble Space Telescope has even helped researchers calculate the age of our universe. Using the HST, astronomers studied **white dwarf stars**. These are stars that have burned out but still give off heat. The astronomers measured the heat coming from these stars and calculated their age to be 12 to 13 billion years old.

Earlier data from the Hubble had shown that the first stars in the universe formed less than 1 billion years after the Big Bang. By adding this number to the age of the white dwarfs, astronomers were able to estimate the age of the universe.

Since January 2002, Hubble has helped scientists study the actions of a star that, for a short time, became 600,000 times brighter than our Sun. For a while, it was the brightest star in the Milky Way. The star has since lost its brightness. However, unlike a dying star, it appears to be expanding. Scientists believe they are witnessing a stage at the end of a star's evolution that is rarely seen. Hubble is capturing the entire process.

SOME OF HUBBLE'S DISCOVERIES

- Showed comet Shoemaker-Levy 9 "attacking" Jupiter
- Revealed two never-before-seen moons orbiting Saturn
- Showed never-before-seen surface details of Pluto
- Took first detailed close-up of a supernova, or exploding star
- Took first detailed close-up of a suspected black hole
- Showed large spiral galaxy NGC 253
- Measured the brightness of many distant stars
- Detected the atmosphere of a planet orbiting a star outside of our solar system
- Helped astronomers determine the age of the universe
- Photographed galaxies 13 billion light-years away from Earth, when the universe was about 1 billion years old
- Showed large spiral galaxy NGC 3949

Hubble's pictures have helped scientists better understand our universe. It has proven the existence of black holes and has shown that galaxies change over time. Scientists also now have an idea of how stars are born and how they die.

In 2002, Hubble beamed down spectacular images of the Cone Nebula. The Cone Nebula is a cloud of gas and dust approximately 2,500 light-years from Earth. Stars were being born within the cloud, and Hubble captured the images.

The Cone Nebula

Even more exciting, Hubble has helped astronomers detect the atmosphere of a planet orbiting around a star outside our solar system. When the planet passed in front of the star, astronomers analyzed Hubble's pictures of the star's light as it passed through the planet's atmosphere. They discovered that there was sodium. Sodium is a chemical element that is present in salt. This discovery opens up the possibility of exploring the atmospheres of planets beyond our solar system for evidence of life beyond Earth.

However, Hubble's days are numbered. It will continue operating only until 2007 or 2008. Eventually, it will become useless. Hubble will fall out of orbit and crash to Earth a few years later. A robot guide will make sure Hubble splashes harmlessly into the ocean.

A bigger, more complex telescope will take Hubble's place in outer space. It has a mirror made of segments and is more than 20 feet in diameter. With this mirror, the James Webb Space Telescope (JWST) will be able to spot objects 400 times more faint than objects that Hubble can detect.

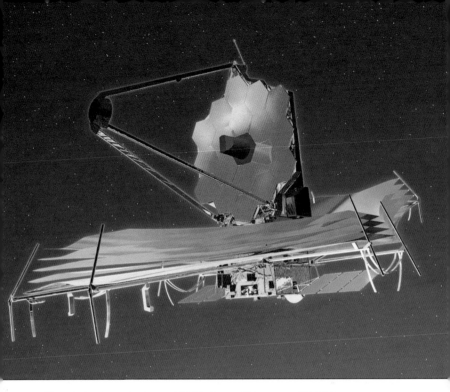

The design for the James Webb Space Telescope (JWST)

The launch of the JWST is planned for 2011. After the launch, a large sunshield will unfold. The sunshield will protect the mirror from the Sun's heat. Scientists hope that the JWST will see galaxies even farther away. The JWST will be responsible for helping scientists to continue to piece together the puzzles of our universe.

GLOSSARY

astronomers scientists who study stars, planets, and other objects in the sky

black holes regions or bodies in space with gravity so strong that neither light nor matter can escape them

cosmos the universe considered as a whole

deployed moved an object, such as a satellite, into position

eclipses partial or complete darkening or hiding of one object by another

galaxies collections of billions of stars and other matter held together by gravity

gravity the force by which all objects in the universe are attracted to each other

light-year the distance that light travels in a year, approximately 6 trillion miles

radio signals electrical impulses with wavelengths less than about $\frac{1}{25}$ of an inch

reflecting telescope a telescope that uses two mirrors to collect and focus light

refracting telescope a telescope that uses two clear glass lenses to collect and focus light

shuttle a bus, airplane, train, or spacecraft that travels the same route back and forth; space shuttles are used over again to carry astronauts and equipment into outer space

solar system a grouping of planets and other celestial bodies that revolve around a star; our solar system is in the Milky Way galaxy

white dwarf stars small, whitish stars that have burned out but have very concentrated mass and still emit heat